FREE LIVING SOUL CARE PLANNER
@2020 by Tracey M. Lewis-Giggetts and NewSeason Books and Media

Free Living is a brand of NewSeason Books and Media

NewSeason Books and Media
PO Box 1403
Havertown, PA 19083
www.nsbooksandmedia.com
newseasonbooks@gmail.com

All rights reserved. No part of this book may be reproduced in any form or by any means including electronic, mechanical or photocopying or stored in a retrieval system without permission in writing from the publisher except by a reviewer who may quote brief passages to be included in a review.

FREE LIVING

A Soul Care Planner

A QUARTERLY QUEST
FOR LIVING WELL

When considering the kind of planner product we'd release this year, I knew I didn't want something that would just help you plan and track productivity. There are a million and one great planners and calendars out there for that. I wanted something that would facilitate a person's healing. Something that would encourage a person to put themselves first; to fill their own cup so they can serve others from their overflow as opposed to walking around on empty. That is the impetus for NSB's Free Living brand and this planner.

My hope and prayer is that you will find this soul care planner to be a much needed companion on your journey toward healing and wellness.

Grace and Peace,
Tracey M. Lewis-Giggetts, MBA, MFA
Chief Creative Officer, NewSeason Books and Media

WEEK 1

DATE
....

To live by grace means to acknowledge my whole life story, the light side and the dark. In admitting my shadow side I learn who I am and what God's grace means.

~Brennan Manning

HOW DO I INTEND TO TAKE CARE OF MYSELF THIS WEEK?

_____
_____
_____
_____
_____
_____
_____
_____
_____
_____

MONDAY   DATE: /   /

Daily Heart Check *(How are you feeling today?)*

BODY | How do I plan to feed my body today?

Meals

Water

Exercise

Others

MIND | How do I plan to feed my mind today?

Books/Articles Read

Podcasts Listened To

Significant Conversations

Others

SPIRIT | How did I feed my spirit today?

Prayer/Meditation

Minutes of Stillness (Yes, do nothing!)

Journaling

Others

TUESDAY   DATE: /   /

Daily Heart Check *(How are you feeling today?)*

BODY | How do I plan to feed my body today?

Meals

Water

Exercise

Others

MIND | How do I plan to feed my mind today?

Books/Articles Read

Podcasts Listened To

Significant Conversations

Others

SPIRIT | How did I feed my spirit today?

Prayer/Meditation

Minutes of Stillness (Yes, do nothing!)

Journaling

Others

WEDNESDAY   DATE: /   /

Daily Heart Check *(How are you feeling today?)*

BODY | How do I plan to feed my body today?

Meals

Water

Exercise

Others

MIND | How do I plan to feed my mind today?

Books/Articles Read

Podcasts Listened To

Significant Conversations

Others

SPIRIT | How did I feed my spirit today?

Prayer/Meditation

Minutes of Stillness (Yes, do nothing!)

Journaling

Others

THURSDAY   DATE: /   /

Daily Heart Check *(How are you feeling today?)*

BODY | How do I plan to feed my body today?

Meals

Water

Exercise

Others

MIND | How do I plan to feed my mind today?

Books/Articles Read

Podcasts Listened To

Significant Conversations

Others

SPIRIT | How did I feed my spirit today?

Prayer/Meditation

Minutes of Stillness (Yes, do nothing!)

Journaling

Others

FRIDAY   DATE: /   /

Daily Heart Check *(How are you feeling today?)*

BODY | How do I plan to feed my body today?

Meals

Water

Exercise

Others

MIND | How do I plan to feed my mind today?

Books/Articles Read

Podcasts Listened To

Significant Conversations

Others

SPIRIT | How did I feed my spirit today?

Prayer/Meditation

Minutes of Stillness (Yes, do nothing!)

Journaling

Others

SATURDAY   DATE: /   /

Daily Heart Check *(How are you feeling today?)*

BODY | How do I plan to feed my body today?

Meals

Water

Exercise

Others

MIND | How do I plan to feed my mind today?

Books/Articles Read

Podcasts Listened To

Significant Conversations

Others

SPIRIT | How did I feed my spirit today?

Prayer/Meditation

Minutes of Stillness (Yes, do nothing!)

Journaling

Others

SUNDAY   DATE: /   /

Daily Heart Check *(How are you feeling today?)*

BODY | How do I plan to feed my body today?

Meals

Water

Exercise

Others

MIND | How do I plan to feed my mind today?

Books/Articles Read

Podcasts Listened To

Significant Conversations

Others

SPIRIT | How did I feed my spirit today?

Prayer/Meditation

Minutes of Stillness (Yes, do nothing!)

Journaling

Others

WINS	AREAS TO WORK ON

Dear me,

NOW...
LET IT GO.

ALL IS WELL.
YOU ARE OKAY.
YOU ARE ENOUGH.
YOU ARE HEALING.

TURN THE PAGE AND
BEGIN AGAIN

WEEK 2

DATE
....

Curate your calendar like it's a sacred space.

~@napministry

HOW DO I INTEND TO TAKE CARE OF MYSELF THIS WEEK?

_____
_____
_____
_____
_____
_____
_____
_____
_____
_____
_____

MONDAY   DATE: /   /

Daily Heart Check *(How are you feeling today?)*

[   ]

BODY | How do I plan to feed my body today?

Meals

Water

Exercise

Others

MIND | How do I plan to feed my mind today?

Books/Articles Read

Podcasts Listened To

Significant Conversations

Others

SPIRIT | How did I feed my spirit today?

Prayer/Meditation

Minutes of Stillness (Yes, do nothing!)

Journaling

Others

TUESDAY   DATE: /   /

Daily Heart Check *(How are you feeling today?)*

BODY | How do I plan to feed my body today?

Meals

Water

Exercise

Others

MIND | How do I plan to feed my mind today?

Books/Articles Read

Podcasts Listened To

Significant Conversations

Others

SPIRIT | How did I feed my spirit today?

Prayer/Meditation

Minutes of Stillness (Yes, do nothing!)

Journaling

Others

WEDNESDAY   DATE: /   /

Daily Heart Check *(How are you feeling today?)*

BODY | How do I plan to feed my body today?

Meals

Water

Exercise

Others

MIND | How do I plan to feed my mind today?

Books/Articles Read

Podcasts Listened To

Significant Conversations

Others

SPIRIT | How did I feed my spirit today?

Prayer/Meditation

Minutes of Stillness (Yes, do nothing!)

Journaling

Others

THURSDAY   DATE: /   /

Daily Heart Check *(How are you feeling today?)*

BODY | How do I plan to feed my body today?

Meals

Water

Exercise

Others

MIND | How do I plan to feed my mind today?

Books/Articles Read

Podcasts Listened To

Significant Conversations

Others

SPIRIT | How did I feed my spirit today?

Prayer/Meditation

Minutes of Stillness (Yes, do nothing!)

Journaling

Others

FRIDAY   DATE: /   /

Daily Heart Check *(How are you feeling today?)*

BODY | How do I plan to feed my body today?

Meals

Water

Exercise

Others

MIND | How do I plan to feed my mind today?

Books/Articles Read

Podcasts Listened To

Significant Conversations

Others

SPIRIT | How did I feed my spirit today?

Prayer/Meditation

Minutes of Stillness (Yes, do nothing!)

Journaling

Others

SATURDAY   DATE: /   /

Daily Heart Check *(How are you feeling today?)*

BODY | How do I plan to feed my body today?

Meals

Water

Exercise

Others

MIND | How do I plan to feed my mind today?

Books/Articles Read

Podcasts Listened To

Significant Conversations

Others

SPIRIT | How did I feed my spirit today?

Prayer/Meditation

Minutes of Stillness (Yes, do nothing!)

Journaling

Others

SUNDAY   DATE: /   /

Daily Heart Check *(How are you feeling today?)*

BODY | How do I plan to feed my body today?

Meals

Water

Exercise

Others

MIND | How do I plan to feed my mind today?

Books/Articles Read

Podcasts Listened To

Significant Conversations

Others

SPIRIT | How did I feed my spirit today?

Prayer/Meditation

Minutes of Stillness (Yes, do nothing!)

Journaling

Others

WINS	AREAS TO WORK ON

Dear me,

NOW...
LET IT GO.

ALL IS WELL.
YOU ARE OKAY.
YOU ARE ENOUGH.
YOU ARE HEALING.

TURN THE PAGE AND BEGIN AGAIN

WEEK 3

DATE
....

The real stuff of life is rarely found in precise moments or noteworthy days, but in the daily walking out of our gradually unfolding stories.

~John Pavlovitz

HOW DO I INTEND TO TAKE CARE OF MYSELF THIS WEEK?

_____
_____
_____
_____
_____
_____
_____
_____
_____
_____

MONDAY   DATE: /   /

Daily Heart Check *(How are you feeling today?)*

BODY | How do I plan to feed my body today?

Meals

Water

Exercise

Others

MIND | How do I plan to feed my mind today?

Books/Articles Read

Podcasts Listened To

Significant Conversations

Others

SPIRIT | How did I feed my spirit today?

Prayer/Meditation

Minutes of Stillness (Yes, do nothing!)

Journaling

Others

TUESDAY   DATE: /   /

Daily Heart Check *(How are you feeling today?)*

```
┌─────────────────────────────────────────────────────────┐
│                                                         │
│                                                         │
│                                                         │
│                                                         │
└─────────────────────────────────────────────────────────┘
```

BODY | How do I plan to feed my body today?

Meals

Water

Exercise

Others

MIND | How do I plan to feed my mind today?

Books/Articles Read

Podcasts Listened To

Significant Conversations

Others

SPIRIT | How did I feed my spirit today?

Prayer/Meditation

Minutes of Stillness (Yes, do nothing!)

Journaling

Others

WEDNESDAY   DATE: /   /

Daily Heart Check *(How are you feeling today?)*

BODY | How do I plan to feed my body today?

Meals

Water

Exercise

Others

MIND | How do I plan to feed my mind today?

Books/Articles Read

Podcasts Listened To

Significant Conversations

Others

SPIRIT | How did I feed my spirit today?

Prayer/Meditation

Minutes of Stillness (Yes, do nothing!)

Journaling

Others

THURSDAY   DATE: /   /

Daily Heart Check *(How are you feeling today?)*

BODY | How do I plan to feed my body today?

Meals

Water

Exercise

Others

MIND | How do I plan to feed my mind today?

Books/Articles Read

Podcasts Listened To

Significant Conversations

Others

SPIRIT | How did I feed my spirit today?

Prayer/Meditation

Minutes of Stillness (Yes, do nothing!)

Journaling

Others

FRIDAY   DATE: /   /

Daily Heart Check *(How are you feeling today?)*

BODY | How do I plan to feed my body today?

Meals

Water

Exercise

Others

MIND | How do I plan to feed my mind today?

Books/Articles Read

Podcasts Listened To

Significant Conversations

Others

SPIRIT | How did I feed my spirit today?

Prayer/Meditation

Minutes of Stillness (Yes, do nothing!)

Journaling

Others

SATURDAY   DATE: /   /

Daily Heart Check *(How are you feeling today?)*

BODY | How do I plan to feed my body today?

Meals

Water

Exercise

Others

MIND | How do I plan to feed my mind today?

Books/Articles Read

Podcasts Listened To

Significant Conversations

Others

SPIRIT | How did I feed my spirit today?

Prayer/Meditation

Minutes of Stillness (Yes, do nothing!)

Journaling

Others

SUNDAY   DATE: /   /

Daily Heart Check *(How are you feeling today?)*

```
┌─────────────────────────────────────────────────────────────┐
│                                                             │
│                                                             │
│                                                             │
└─────────────────────────────────────────────────────────────┘
```

BODY | How do I plan to feed my body today?

Meals
_____

Water
_____

Exercise
_____

Others
_____

MIND | How do I plan to feed my mind today?

Books/Articles Read
_____

Podcasts Listened To
_____

Significant Conversations
_____

Others
_____

SPIRIT | How did I feed my spirit today?

Prayer/Meditation
_____

Minutes of Stillness (Yes, do nothing!)
_____

Journaling
_____

Others
_____

WINS	AREAS TO WORK ON

Dear me,

NOW...
LET IT GO.

ALL IS WELL.

YOU ARE OKAY.

YOU ARE ENOUGH.

YOU ARE HEALING.

TURN THE PAGE AND
BEGIN AGAIN

WEEK 4

DATE

No person is your friend who demands your silence, or denies your right to grow.

~Alice Walker

HOW DO I INTEND TO TAKE CARE OF MYSELF THIS WEEK?

_____
_____
_____
_____
_____
_____
_____
_____
_____
_____

MONDAY   DATE: /   /

Daily Heart Check *(How are you feeling today?)*

[   ]

BODY | How do I plan to feed my body today?

Meals

Water

Exercise

Others

MIND | How do I plan to feed my mind today?

Books/Articles Read

Podcasts Listened To

Significant Conversations

Others

SPIRIT | How did I feed my spirit today?

Prayer/Meditation

Minutes of Stillness (Yes, do nothing!)

Journaling

Others

TUESDAY   DATE: /   /

Daily Heart Check *(How are you feeling today?)*

BODY | How do I plan to feed my body today?

Meals

Water

Exercise

Others

MIND | How do I plan to feed my mind today?

Books/Articles Read

Podcasts Listened To

Significant Conversations

Others

SPIRIT | How did I feed my spirit today?

Prayer/Meditation

Minutes of Stillness (Yes, do nothing!)

Journaling

Others

WEDNESDAY   DATE: /   /

Daily Heart Check *(How are you feeling today?)*

BODY | How do I plan to feed my body today?

Meals

Water

Exercise

Others

MIND | How do I plan to feed my mind today?

Books/Articles Read

Podcasts Listened To

Significant Conversations

Others

SPIRIT | How did I feed my spirit today?

Prayer/Meditation

Minutes of Stillness (Yes, do nothing!)

Journaling

Others

THURSDAY   DATE: /   /

Daily Heart Check *(How are you feeling today?)*

BODY | How do I plan to feed my body today?

Meals

Water

Exercise

Others

MIND | How do I plan to feed my mind today?

Books/Articles Read

Podcasts Listened To

Significant Conversations

Others

SPIRIT | How did I feed my spirit today?

Prayer/Meditation

Minutes of Stillness (Yes, do nothing!)

Journaling

Others

FRIDAY   DATE: /   /

Daily Heart Check *(How are you feeling today?)*

BODY | How do I plan to feed my body today?

Meals

Water

Exercise

Others

MIND | How do I plan to feed my mind today?

Books/Articles Read

Podcasts Listened To

Significant Conversations

Others

SPIRIT | How did I feed my spirit today?

Prayer/Meditation

Minutes of Stillness (Yes, do nothing!)

Journaling

Others

SATURDAY   DATE: /   /

Daily Heart Check *(How are you feeling today?)*

BODY | How do I plan to feed my body today?

Meals

Water

Exercise

Others

MIND | How do I plan to feed my mind today?

Books/Articles Read

Podcasts Listened To

Significant Conversations

Others

SPIRIT | How did I feed my spirit today?

Prayer/Meditation

Minutes of Stillness (Yes, do nothing!)

Journaling

Others

SUNDAY   DATE: /   /

Daily Heart Check *(How are you feeling today?)*

```
┌─────────────────────────────────────────────────────────────────────┐
│                                                                     │
│                                                                     │
│                                                                     │
│                                                                     │
└─────────────────────────────────────────────────────────────────────┘
```

BODY | How do I plan to feed my body today?

Meals

Water

Exercise

Others

MIND | How do I plan to feed my mind today?

Books/Articles Read

Podcasts Listened To

Significant Conversations

Others

SPIRIT | How did I feed my spirit today?

Prayer/Meditation

Minutes of Stillness (Yes, do nothing!)

Journaling

Others

WINS	AREAS TO WORK ON

Dear me,

NOW...
LET IT GO.

ALL IS WELL.
YOU ARE OKAY.
YOU ARE ENOUGH.
YOU ARE HEALING.

TURN THE PAGE AND
BEGIN AGAIN

WEEK 5

DATE
....

We must grapple with our fear if we are ever going to come to a place of love.

~Christena Cleveland

HOW DO I INTEND TO TAKE CARE OF MYSELF THIS WEEK?

_____
_____
_____
_____
_____
_____
_____
_____
_____
_____

MONDAY															DATE:	 /	 /

Daily Heart Check *(How are you feeling today?)*

BODY | How do I plan to feed my body today?

Meals

Water

Exercise

Others

MIND | How do I plan to feed my mind today?

Books/Articles Read

Podcasts Listened To

Significant Conversations

Others

SPIRIT | How did I feed my spirit today?

Prayer/Meditation

Minutes of Stillness (Yes, do nothing!)

Journaling

Others

TUESDAY   DATE: /   /

Daily Heart Check *(How are you feeling today?)*

BODY | How do I plan to feed my body today?

Meals

Water

Exercise

Others

MIND | How do I plan to feed my mind today?

Books/Articles Read

Podcasts Listened To

Significant Conversations

Others

SPIRIT | How did I feed my spirit today?

Prayer/Meditation

Minutes of Stillness (Yes, do nothing!)

Journaling

Others

WEDNESDAY DATE: /   /

Daily Heart Check *(How are you feeling today?)*

BODY | How do I plan to feed my body today?

Meals

Water

Exercise

Others

MIND | How do I plan to feed my mind today?

Books/Articles Read

Podcasts Listened To

Significant Conversations

Others

SPIRIT | How did I feed my spirit today?

Prayer/Meditation

Minutes of Stillness (Yes, do nothing!)

Journaling

Others

THURSDAY   DATE: /   /

Daily Heart Check *(How are you feeling today?)*

BODY | How do I plan to feed my body today?

Meals

Water

Exercise

Others

MIND | How do I plan to feed my mind today?

Books/Articles Read

Podcasts Listened To

Significant Conversations

Others

SPIRIT | How did I feed my spirit today?

Prayer/Meditation

Minutes of Stillness (Yes, do nothing!)

Journaling

Others

FRIDAY   DATE: /   /

Daily Heart Check *(How are you feeling today?)*

BODY | How do I plan to feed my body today?

Meals

Water

Exercise

Others

MIND | How do I plan to feed my mind today?

Books/Articles Read

Podcasts Listened To

Significant Conversations

Others

SPIRIT | How did I feed my spirit today?

Prayer/Meditation

Minutes of Stillness (Yes, do nothing!)

Journaling

Others

SATURDAY   DATE: /   /

Daily Heart Check *(How are you feeling today?)*

BODY | How do I plan to feed my body today?

Meals

Water

Exercise

Others

MIND | How do I plan to feed my mind today?

Books/Articles Read

Podcasts Listened To

Significant Conversations

Others

SPIRIT | How did I feed my spirit today?

Prayer/Meditation

Minutes of Stillness (Yes, do nothing!)

Journaling

Others

SUNDAY   DATE: /   /

Daily Heart Check *(How are you feeling today?)*

[   ]

BODY | How do I plan to feed my body today?

Meals

Water

Exercise

Others

MIND | How do I plan to feed my mind today?

Books/Articles Read

Podcasts Listened To

Significant Conversations

Others

SPIRIT | How did I feed my spirit today?

Prayer/Meditation

Minutes of Stillness (Yes, do nothing!)

Journaling

Others

WINS	AREAS TO WORK ON

Dear me,

NOW...
LET IT GO.

ALL IS WELL.
YOU ARE OKAY.
YOU ARE ENOUGH.
YOU ARE HEALING.

TURN THE PAGE AND BEGIN AGAIN

WEEK 6

DATE
....

Do what you can, with what you have, where you are.

~Theodore Roosevelt

HOW DO I INTEND TO TAKE CARE OF MYSELF THIS WEEK?

_____
_____
_____
_____
_____
_____
_____
_____
_____
_____
_____

MONDAY   DATE: /   /

Daily Heart Check *(How are you feeling today?)*

```
┌─────────────────────────────────────────────────────────────┐
│                                                             │
│                                                             │
│                                                             │
│                                                             │
└─────────────────────────────────────────────────────────────┘
```

BODY | How do I plan to feed my body today?

Meals
_____

Water
_____

Exercise
_____

Others
_____

MIND | How do I plan to feed my mind today?

Books/Articles Read
_____

Podcasts Listened To
_____

Significant Conversations
_____

Others
_____

SPIRIT | How did I feed my spirit today?

Prayer/Meditation
_____

Minutes of Stillness (Yes, do nothing!)
_____

Journaling
_____

Others
_____

TUESDAY   DATE: /   /

Daily Heart Check *(How are you feeling today?)*

BODY | How do I plan to feed my body today?

Meals

Water

Exercise

Others

MIND | How do I plan to feed my mind today?

Books/Articles Read

Podcasts Listened To

Significant Conversations

Others

SPIRIT | How did I feed my spirit today?

Prayer/Meditation

Minutes of Stillness (Yes, do nothing!)

Journaling

Others

WEDNESDAY   DATE: /   /

Daily Heart Check *(How are you feeling today?)*

BODY | How do I plan to feed my body today?

Meals

Water

Exercise

Others

MIND | How do I plan to feed my mind today?

Books/Articles Read

Podcasts Listened To

Significant Conversations

Others

SPIRIT | How did I feed my spirit today?

Prayer/Meditation

Minutes of Stillness (Yes, do nothing!)

Journaling

Others

THURSDAY   DATE: /   /

Daily Heart Check *(How are you feeling today?)*

BODY | How do I plan to feed my body today?

Meals

Water

Exercise

Others

MIND | How do I plan to feed my mind today?

Books/Articles Read

Podcasts Listened To

Significant Conversations

Others

SPIRIT | How did I feed my spirit today?

Prayer/Meditation

Minutes of Stillness (Yes, do nothing!)

Journaling

Others

FRIDAY   DATE: /   /

Daily Heart Check *(How are you feeling today?)*

```
........................................................................
:                                                                      :
:                                                                      :
:                                                                      :
:                                                                      :
:                                                                      :
........................................................................
```

BODY | How do I plan to feed my body today?

Meals
_____

Water
_____

Exercise
_____

Others
_____

MIND | How do I plan to feed my mind today?

Books/Articles Read
_____

Podcasts Listened To
_____

Significant Conversations
_____

Others
_____

SPIRIT | How did I feed my spirit today?

Prayer/Meditation
_____

Minutes of Stillness (Yes, do nothing!)
_____

Journaling
_____

Others
_____

SATURDAY   DATE: /   /

Daily Heart Check *(How are you feeling today?)*

BODY | How do I plan to feed my body today?

Meals

Water

Exercise

Others

MIND | How do I plan to feed my mind today?

Books/Articles Read

Podcasts Listened To

Significant Conversations

Others

SPIRIT | How did I feed my spirit today?

Prayer/Meditation

Minutes of Stillness (Yes, do nothing!)

Journaling

Others

SUNDAY   DATE: /   /

Daily Heart Check *(How are you feeling today?)*

BODY | How do I plan to feed my body today?

Meals

Water

Exercise

Others

MIND | How do I plan to feed my mind today?

Books/Articles Read

Podcasts Listened To

Significant Conversations

Others

SPIRIT | How did I feed my spirit today?

Prayer/Meditation

Minutes of Stillness (Yes, do nothing!)

Journaling

Others

WINS	AREAS TO WORK ON

Dear me,

NOW...
LET IT GO.

ALL IS WELL.
YOU ARE OKAY.
YOU ARE ENOUGH.
YOU ARE HEALING.

TURN THE PAGE AND BEGIN AGAIN

WEEK 7

DATE
....

Never be afraid to sit awhile and think.

~Lorraine Hansberry

HOW DO I INTEND TO TAKE CARE OF MYSELF THIS WEEK?

_____
_____
_____
_____
_____
_____
_____
_____
_____
_____
_____
_____

MONDAY   DATE: /   /

Daily Heart Check *(How are you feeling today?)*

[   ]

BODY | How do I plan to feed my body today?

Meals

Water

Exercise

Others

MIND | How do I plan to feed my mind today?

Books/Articles Read

Podcasts Listened To

Significant Conversations

Others

SPIRIT | How did I feed my spirit today?

TUESDAY   DATE: /   /

Daily Heart Check *(How are you feeling today?)*

BODY | How do I plan to feed my body today?

Meals

Water

Exercise

Others

MIND | How do I plan to feed my mind today?

Books/Articles Read

Podcasts Listened To

Significant Conversations

Others

SPIRIT | How did I feed my spirit today?

WEDNESDAY   DATE: /   /

Daily Heart Check *(How are you feeling today?)*

BODY | How do I plan to feed my body today?

Meals

Water

Exercise

Others

MIND | How do I plan to feed my mind today?

Books/Articles Read

Podcasts Listened To

Significant Conversations

Others

SPIRIT | How did I feed my spirit today?

THURSDAY   DATE: /   /

Daily Heart Check *(How are you feeling today?)*

BODY | How do I plan to feed my body today?

Meals

Water

Exercise

Others

MIND | How do I plan to feed my mind today?

Books/Articles Read

Podcasts Listened To

Significant Conversations

Others

SPIRIT | How did I feed my spirit today?

Prayer/Meditation

Minutes of Stillness (Yes, do nothing!)

Journaling

Others

FRIDAY   DATE: /   /

Daily Heart Check *(How are you feeling today?)*

BODY | How do I plan to feed my body today?

Meals

Water

Exercise

Others

MIND | How do I plan to feed my mind today?

Books/Articles Read

Podcasts Listened To

Significant Conversations

Others

SPIRIT | How did I feed my spirit today?

Prayer/Meditation

Minutes of Stillness (Yes, do nothing!)

Journaling

Others

SATURDAY   DATE: /   /

Daily Heart Check *(How are you feeling today?)*

BODY | How do I plan to feed my body today?

Meals

Water

Exercise

Others

MIND | How do I plan to feed my mind today?

Books/Articles Read

Podcasts Listened To

Significant Conversations

Others

SPIRIT | How did I feed my spirit today?

Prayer/Meditation

Minutes of Stillness (Yes, do nothing!)

Journaling

Others

SUNDAY					DATE: / /

Daily Heart Check *(How are you feeling today?)*

BODY | How do I plan to feed my body today?

Meals

Water

Exercise

Others

MIND | How do I plan to feed my mind today?

Books/Articles Read

Podcasts Listened To

Significant Conversations

Others

SPIRIT | How did I feed my spirit today?

Prayer/Meditation

Minutes of Stillness (Yes, do nothing!)

Journaling

Others

WINS	AREAS TO WORK ON

Dear me,

NOW...
LET IT GO.

ALL IS WELL.
YOU ARE OKAY.
YOU ARE ENOUGH.
YOU ARE HEALING.

TURN THE PAGE AND BEGIN AGAIN

WEEK 8

DATE
....

Do I contradict myself? Very well, then, I contradict myself; I am large -- I contain multitudes.

~Walt Whitman

HOW DO I INTEND TO TAKE CARE OF MYSELF THIS WEEK?

_____
_____
_____
_____
_____
_____
_____
_____
_____
_____

MONDAY																												DATE: / /

Daily Heart Check *(How are you feeling today?)*

BODY | How do I plan to feed my body today?

Meals

Water

Exercise

Others

MIND | How do I plan to feed my mind today?

Books/Articles Read

Podcasts Listened To

Significant Conversations

Others

SPIRIT | How did I feed my spirit today?

Prayer/Meditation

Minutes of Stillness (Yes, do nothing!)

Journaling

Others

TUESDAY   DATE: /   /

Daily Heart Check *(How are you feeling today?)*

[   ]

BODY | How do I plan to feed my body today?

Meals

Water

Exercise

Others

MIND | How do I plan to feed my mind today?

Books/Articles Read

Podcasts Listened To

Significant Conversations

Others

SPIRIT | How did I feed my spirit today?

Prayer/Meditation

Minutes of Stillness (Yes, do nothing!)

Journaling

Others

WEDNESDAY   DATE: /   /

Daily Heart Check *(How are you feeling today?)*

BODY | How do I plan to feed my body today?

Meals

Water

Exercise

Others

MIND | How do I plan to feed my mind today?

Books/Articles Read

Podcasts Listened To

Significant Conversations

Others

SPIRIT | How did I feed my spirit today?

Prayer/Meditation

Minutes of Stillness (Yes, do nothing!)

Journaling

Others

THURSDAY   DATE: /   /

Daily Heart Check *(How are you feeling today?)*

BODY | How do I plan to feed my body today?

Meals

Water

Exercise

Others

MIND | How do I plan to feed my mind today?

Books/Articles Read

Podcasts Listened To

Significant Conversations

Others

SPIRIT | How did I feed my spirit today?

Prayer/Meditation

Minutes of Stillness (Yes, do nothing!)

Journaling

Others

FRIDAY   DATE: /   /

Daily Heart Check *(How are you feeling today?)*

BODY | How do I plan to feed my body today?

Meals

Water

Exercise

Others

MIND | How do I plan to feed my mind today?

Books/Articles Read

Podcasts Listened To

Significant Conversations

Others

SPIRIT | How did I feed my spirit today?

Prayer/Meditation

Minutes of Stillness (Yes, do nothing!)

Journaling

Others

SATURDAY   DATE: /   /

Daily Heart Check *(How are you feeling today?)*

BODY | How do I plan to feed my body today?

Meals

Water

Exercise

Others

MIND | How do I plan to feed my mind today?

Books/Articles Read

Podcasts Listened To

Significant Conversations

Others

SPIRIT | How did I feed my spirit today?

Prayer/Meditation

Minutes of Stillness (Yes, do nothing!)

Journaling

Others

SUNDAY   DATE: /   /

Daily Heart Check *(How are you feeling today?)*

BODY | How do I plan to feed my body today?

Meals

Water

Exercise

Others

MIND | How do I plan to feed my mind today?

Books/Articles Read

Podcasts Listened To

Significant Conversations

Others

SPIRIT | How did I feed my spirit today?

Prayer/Meditation

Minutes of Stillness (Yes, do nothing!)

Journaling

Others

WINS	AREAS TO WORK ON

Dear me,

NOW...
LET IT GO.

ALL IS WELL.
YOU ARE OKAY.
YOU ARE ENOUGH.
YOU ARE HEALING.

TURN THE PAGE AND BEGIN AGAIN

WEEK 9

DATE
....

I have discovered in life that there are ways of getting almost anywhere you want to go, if you really want to go.

~Langston Hughes

HOW DO I INTEND TO TAKE CARE OF MYSELF THIS WEEK?

_____
_____
_____
_____
_____
_____
_____
_____
_____
_____
_____
_____

MONDAY   DATE: /   /

Daily Heart Check *(How are you feeling today?)*

[   ]

BODY | How do I plan to feed my body today?

Meals

Water

Exercise

Others

MIND | How do I plan to feed my mind today?

Books/Articles Read

Podcasts Listened To

Significant Conversations

Others

SPIRIT | How did I feed my spirit today?

Prayer/Meditation

Minutes of Stillness (Yes, do nothing!)

Journaling

Others

TUESDAY   DATE: /   /

Daily Heart Check *(How are you feeling today?)*

BODY | How do I plan to feed my body today?

Meals

Water

Exercise

Others

MIND | How do I plan to feed my mind today?

Books/Articles Read

Podcasts Listened To

Significant Conversations

Others

SPIRIT | How did I feed my spirit today?

Prayer/Meditation

Minutes of Stillness (Yes, do nothing!)

Journaling

Others

WEDNESDAY   DATE: /   /

Daily Heart Check *(How are you feeling today?)*

BODY | How do I plan to feed my body today?

Meals

Water

Exercise

Others

MIND | How do I plan to feed my mind today?

Books/Articles Read

Podcasts Listened To

Significant Conversations

Others

SPIRIT | How did I feed my spirit today?

Prayer/Meditation

Minutes of Stillness (Yes, do nothing!)

Journaling

Others

THURSDAY   DATE: /   /

Daily Heart Check *(How are you feeling today?)*

BODY | How do I plan to feed my body today?

Meals

Water

Exercise

Others

MIND | How do I plan to feed my mind today?

Books/Articles Read

Podcasts Listened To

Significant Conversations

Others

SPIRIT | How did I feed my spirit today?

Prayer/Meditation

Minutes of Stillness (Yes, do nothing!)

Journaling

Others

FRIDAY   DATE: /   /

Daily Heart Check *(How are you feeling today?)*

BODY | How do I plan to feed my body today?

Meals

Water

Exercise

Others

MIND | How do I plan to feed my mind today?

Books/Articles Read

Podcasts Listened To

Significant Conversations

Others

SPIRIT | How did I feed my spirit today?

Prayer/Meditation

Minutes of Stillness (Yes, do nothing!)

Journaling

Others

SATURDAY   DATE: /   /

Daily Heart Check *(How are you feeling today?)*

BODY | How do I plan to feed my body today?

Meals

Water

Exercise

Others

MIND | How do I plan to feed my mind today?

Books/Articles Read

Podcasts Listened To

Significant Conversations

Others

SPIRIT | How did I feed my spirit today?

Prayer/Meditation

Minutes of Stillness (Yes, do nothing!)

Journaling

Others

SUNDAY   DATE: /   /

Daily Heart Check *(How are you feeling today?)*

[   ]

BODY | How do I plan to feed my body today?

Meals

Water

Exercise

Others

MIND | How do I plan to feed my mind today?

Books/Articles Read

Podcasts Listened To

Significant Conversations

Others

SPIRIT | How did I feed my spirit today?

Prayer/Meditation

Minutes of Stillness (Yes, do nothing!)

Journaling

Others

WINS	AREAS TO WORK ON

Dear me,

NOW...
LET IT GO.

ALL IS WELL.
YOU ARE OKAY.
YOU ARE ENOUGH.
YOU ARE HEALING.

TURN THE PAGE AND
BEGIN AGAIN

WEEK 10

DATE
....

Breathe. Let go. And remind yourself that this very moment is the only one you know you have for sure.

~Oprah Winfrey

HOW DO I INTEND TO TAKE CARE OF MYSELF THIS WEEK?

_____
_____
_____
_____
_____
_____
_____
_____
_____
_____
_____

MONDAY   DATE: /   /

Daily Heart Check *(How are you feeling today?)*

BODY | How do I plan to feed my body today?

Meals

Water

Exercise

Others

MIND | How do I plan to feed my mind today?

Books/Articles Read

Podcasts Listened To

Significant Conversations

Others

SPIRIT | How did I feed my spirit today?

Prayer/Meditation

Minutes of Stillness (Yes, do nothing!)

Journaling

Others

TUESDAY   DATE: /   /

Daily Heart Check *(How are you feeling today?)*

BODY | How do I plan to feed my body today?

Meals

Water

Exercise

Others

MIND | How do I plan to feed my mind today?

Books/Articles Read

Podcasts Listened To

Significant Conversations

Others

SPIRIT | How did I feed my spirit today?

Prayer/Meditation

Minutes of Stillness (Yes, do nothing!)

Journaling

Others

WEDNESDAY   DATE: /   /

Daily Heart Check *(How are you feeling today?)*

```
................................................................
:                                                              :
:                                                              :
:                                                              :
:                                                              :
:                                                              :
................................................................
```

BODY | How do I plan to feed my body today?

Meals
_____

Water
_____

Exercise
_____

Others
_____

MIND | How do I plan to feed my mind today?

Books/Articles Read
_____

Podcasts Listened To
_____

Significant Conversations
_____

Others
_____

SPIRIT | How did I feed my spirit today?

Prayer/Meditation
_____

Minutes of Stillness (Yes, do nothing!)
_____

Journaling
_____

Others
_____

THURSDAY   DATE: /   /

Daily Heart Check *(How are you feeling today?)*

BODY | How do I plan to feed my body today?

Meals

Water

Exercise

Others

MIND | How do I plan to feed my mind today?

Books/Articles Read

Podcasts Listened To

Significant Conversations

Others

SPIRIT | How did I feed my spirit today?

Prayer/Meditation

Minutes of Stillness (Yes, do nothing!)

Journaling

Others

FRIDAY   DATE: /   /

Daily Heart Check *(How are you feeling today?)*

BODY | How do I plan to feed my body today?

Meals

Water

Exercise

Others

MIND | How do I plan to feed my mind today?

Books/Articles Read

Podcasts Listened To

Significant Conversations

Others

SPIRIT | How did I feed my spirit today?

Prayer/Meditation

Minutes of Stillness (Yes, do nothing!)

Journaling

Others

SATURDAY   DATE: /   /

Daily Heart Check *(How are you feeling today?)*

BODY | How do I plan to feed my body today?

Meals

Water

Exercise

Others

MIND | How do I plan to feed my mind today?

Books/Articles Read

Podcasts Listened To

Significant Conversations

Others

SPIRIT | How did I feed my spirit today?

Prayer/Meditation

Minutes of Stillness (Yes, do nothing!)

Journaling

Others

SUNDAY   DATE: /   /

Daily Heart Check *(How are you feeling today?)*

BODY | How do I plan to feed my body today?

Meals

Water

Exercise

Others

MIND | How do I plan to feed my mind today?

Books/Articles Read

Podcasts Listened To

Significant Conversations

Others

SPIRIT | How did I feed my spirit today?

Prayer/Meditation

Minutes of Stillness (Yes, do nothing!)

Journaling

Others

WINS	AREAS TO WORK ON

Dear me,
___

NOW...
LET IT GO.

ALL IS WELL.
YOU ARE OKAY.
YOU ARE ENOUGH.
YOU ARE HEALING.

TURN THE PAGE AND BEGIN AGAIN

WEEK 11

DATE
....

When I dare to be powerful to use my strength in the service of my vision, then it becomes less and less important whether I am afraid.

~Audre Lorde

HOW DO I INTEND TO TAKE CARE OF MYSELF THIS WEEK?

_____
_____
_____
_____
_____
_____
_____
_____
_____
_____
_____

MONDAY   DATE: /   /

Daily Heart Check *(How are you feeling today?)*

BODY | How do I plan to feed my body today?

Meals

Water

Exercise

Others

MIND | How do I plan to feed my mind today?

Books/Articles Read

Podcasts Listened To

Significant Conversations

Others

SPIRIT | How did I feed my spirit today?

Prayer/Meditation

Minutes of Stillness (Yes, do nothing!)

Journaling

Others

TUESDAY   DATE: /   /

Daily Heart Check *(How are you feeling today?)*

```
................................................................................
:                                                                              :
:                                                                              :
:                                                                              :
:                                                                              :
:                                                                              :
................................................................................
```

BODY | How do I plan to feed my body today?

Meals

Water

Exercise

Others

MIND | How do I plan to feed my mind today?

Books/Articles Read

Podcasts Listened To

Significant Conversations

Others

SPIRIT | How did I feed my spirit today?

Prayer/Meditation

Minutes of Stillness (Yes, do nothing!)

Journaling

Others

WEDNESDAY   DATE: /   /

Daily Heart Check *(How are you feeling today?)*

BODY | How do I plan to feed my body today?

Meals

Water

Exercise

Others

MIND | How do I plan to feed my mind today?

Books/Articles Read

Podcasts Listened To

Significant Conversations

Others

SPIRIT | How did I feed my spirit today?

Prayer/Meditation

Minutes of Stillness (Yes, do nothing!)

Journaling

Others

THURSDAY   DATE: /   /

Daily Heart Check *(How are you feeling today?)*

BODY | How do I plan to feed my body today?

Meals

Water

Exercise

Others

MIND | How do I plan to feed my mind today?

Books/Articles Read

Podcasts Listened To

Significant Conversations

Others

SPIRIT | How did I feed my spirit today?

Prayer/Meditation

Minutes of Stillness (Yes, do nothing!)

Journaling

Others

FRIDAY   DATE: /   /

Daily Heart Check *(How are you feeling today?)*

BODY | How do I plan to feed my body today?

Meals

Water

Exercise

Others

MIND | How do I plan to feed my mind today?

Books/Articles Read

Podcasts Listened To

Significant Conversations

Others

SPIRIT | How did I feed my spirit today?

Prayer/Meditation

Minutes of Stillness (Yes, do nothing!)

Journaling

Others

SATURDAY   DATE: /   /

Daily Heart Check *(How are you feeling today?)*

BODY | How do I plan to feed my body today?

Meals

Water

Exercise

Others

MIND | How do I plan to feed my mind today?

Books/Articles Read

Podcasts Listened To

Significant Conversations

Others

SPIRIT | How did I feed my spirit today?

Prayer/Meditation

Minutes of Stillness (Yes, do nothing!)

Journaling

Others

SUNDAY   DATE: /   /

Daily Heart Check *(How are you feeling today?)*

```
┌─────────────────────────────────────────────────────────────────┐
│                                                                 │
│                                                                 │
│                                                                 │
│                                                                 │
└─────────────────────────────────────────────────────────────────┘
```

BODY | How do I plan to feed my body today?

Meals

Water

Exercise

Others

MIND | How do I plan to feed my mind today?

Books/Articles Read

Podcasts Listened To

Significant Conversations

Others

SPIRIT | How did I feed my spirit today?

Prayer/Meditation

Minutes of Stillness (Yes, do nothing!)

Journaling

Others

WINS	AREAS TO WORK ON

Dear me,
_____
_____
_____
_____
_____
_____
_____
_____
_____
_____
_____
_____
_____
_____
_____
_____
_____

NOW...
LET IT GO.

ALL IS WELL.
YOU ARE OKAY.
YOU ARE ENOUGH.
YOU ARE HEALING.

**TURN THE PAGE AND
BEGIN AGAIN**

WEEK 12

DATE
....

Freeing yourself was one thing; claiming ownership of that freed self was another.

~Toni Morrison

HOW DO I INTEND TO TAKE CARE OF MYSELF THIS WEEK?

_____
_____
_____
_____
_____
_____
_____
_____
_____
_____
_____
_____

MONDAY   DATE: /   /

Daily Heart Check *(How are you feeling today?)*

BODY | How do I plan to feed my body today?

Meals

Water

Exercise

Others

MIND | How do I plan to feed my mind today?

Books/Articles Read

Podcasts Listened To

Significant Conversations

Others

SPIRIT | How did I feed my spirit today?

Prayer/Meditation

Minutes of Stillness (Yes, do nothing!)

Journaling

Others

TUESDAY   DATE: /   /

Daily Heart Check *(How are you feeling today?)*

[   ]

BODY | How do I plan to feed my body today?

Meals

Water

Exercise

Others

MIND | How do I plan to feed my mind today?

Books/Articles Read

Podcasts Listened To

Significant Conversations

Others

SPIRIT | How did I feed my spirit today?

Prayer/Meditation

Minutes of Stillness (Yes, do nothing!)

Journaling

Others

WEDNESDAY   DATE: /   /

Daily Heart Check *(How are you feeling today?)*

BODY | How do I plan to feed my body today?

Meals

Water

Exercise

Others

MIND | How do I plan to feed my mind today?

Books/Articles Read

Podcasts Listened To

Significant Conversations

Others

SPIRIT | How did I feed my spirit today?

Prayer/Meditation

Minutes of Stillness (Yes, do nothing!)

Journaling

Others

THURSDAY   DATE: /   /

Daily Heart Check *(How are you feeling today?)*

BODY | How do I plan to feed my body today?

Meals

Water

Exercise

Others

MIND | How do I plan to feed my mind today?

Books/Articles Read

Podcasts Listened To

Significant Conversations

Others

SPIRIT | How did I feed my spirit today?

Prayer/Meditation

Minutes of Stillness (Yes, do nothing!)

Journaling

Others

FRIDAY   DATE: /   /

Daily Heart Check *(How are you feeling today?)*

BODY | How do I plan to feed my body today?

Meals

Water

Exercise

Others

MIND | How do I plan to feed my mind today?

Books/Articles Read

Podcasts Listened To

Significant Conversations

Others

SPIRIT | How did I feed my spirit today?

Prayer/Meditation

Minutes of Stillness (Yes, do nothing!)

Journaling

Others

SATURDAY   DATE: /   /

Daily Heart Check *(How are you feeling today?)*

```
┌─────────────────────────────────────────────────────────────┐
│                                                             │
│                                                             │
│                                                             │
│                                                             │
└─────────────────────────────────────────────────────────────┘
```

BODY | How do I plan to feed my body today?

Meals

Water

Exercise

Others

MIND | How do I plan to feed my mind today?

Books/Articles Read

Podcasts Listened To

Significant Conversations

Others

SPIRIT | How did I feed my spirit today?

Prayer/Meditation

Minutes of Stillness (Yes, do nothing!)

Journaling

Others

SUNDAY   DATE: /   /

Daily Heart Check *(How are you feeling today?)*

BODY | How do I plan to feed my body today?

Meals

Water

Exercise

Others

MIND | How do I plan to feed my mind today?

Books/Articles Read

Podcasts Listened To

Significant Conversations

Others

SPIRIT | How did I feed my spirit today?

Prayer/Meditation

Minutes of Stillness (Yes, do nothing!)

Journaling

Others

WINS	AREAS TO WORK ON

Dear me,

NOW...
LET IT GO.

ALL IS WELL.
YOU ARE OKAY.
YOU ARE ENOUGH.
YOU ARE HEALING.

TURN THE PAGE AND BEGIN AGAIN

LIFE ASSESSMENT

It's important to take inventory at the end of these 12 weeks.
Answer the following questions in preparation for moving forward.

What worked for you during this time period and why?

What didn't work for you during this time period and why?

Were there any events or circumstances that hindered your ability
to care for yourself in the way that you hoped?

What intention or goals do you plan to carry into the next quarter?

www.ingramcontent.com/pod-product-compliance
Lightning Source LLC
Chambersburg PA
CBHW081230080526
44587CB00022B/3884